Disabilities and Differences

We All Move

Rebecca Rissman

Heinemann Library
Chicago, Illinois

Customer Service 888-454-2279
Visit our website at www.heinemannraintree.com

Printed in China by South China Printing Company Limited

13 12 11 10 09
10 9 8 7 6 5 4 3 2 1

Library of Congress Cataloging-in-Publication Data
Rissman, Rebecca.
We all move / Rebecca Rissman.
p. cm. -- (Disabilities and differences)
Includes bibliographical references and index.
ISBN 978-1-4329-2150-7 (hc) -- ISBN 978-1-4329-2156-9 (pb) 1. People with disabilities--Orientation and mobility--Juvenile literature. I. Title.
HV3022.R57 2009
612--dc22
                              2008029748

Acknowledgments
The author and publisher are grateful to the following for permission to reproduce copyright material: ©agefotostock p. 4 (Bigshots); ©drr.net pp. 8 (PAGE ONE), 16 (Ronald de Hommel), 20 (Stuart Freedman) 23 middle (PAGE ONE); ©Getty Images pp. 6 (AFP/TEH ENG KOON), 7 (Patrick Byrd), 11 (China Photos), 12 (Brian Bahr), 14 (Doug Pensinger), 15 (Realistic Reflections), 21 (NBAE/Gergory Shamus), 22 (Amy Toensing), 23 bottom (Brian Bahr); ©Jupiter Images pp. 18 (Marc Romanelli), 19 (Thinkstock Images), 23 middle (Thinkstock Images); ©Landov p. 10 (REUTERS/Tony Gentile); ©shutterstock pp. 9 (dellison), 13 (Danny Warren), 17 (felix casio), 23 top (dellison).

Cover image used with permission of ©drr.net (George S de Blonsky). Back cover image used with permission of ©Realistic Reflections (Getty Images).

Every effort has been made to contact copyright holders of any material reproduced in this book. Any omissions will be rectified in subsequent printings if notice is given to the publisher.

Contents

Differences

We are all different.

How Do We Move?

People move in different ways.

People move to go places.

Ways We Move

Some people run.

Some people walk.

Some people dance.

Some people swim.

Some people race.

Some people climb.

Some people ski.

Some people ride.

Some people jump.

Some people swing.

Why Do We Move?

People move to be healthy.

People move to be strong.

Some people move to laugh.

People move to play.

We Are All Different

We are all different.
How do you move?

Words to Know

cane a pole some people use to walk

prosthesis human-made body part. People use prostheses.

wheelchair a chair with wheels. Some people use wheelchairs to get around.

This section includes related vocabulary words that can help students learn about this topic. Use these words to explore movement.

Index

Note to Parents and Teachers

Before reading
Talk with children about the ways we are the same and different. Discuss how some of the differences are physical or mental and some are because different people like different things, but that all people are special and all people are equally important.

After reading
Encourage children to brainstorm different ways to move. Make a list of their suggestions on the board. Then go outside or in the hall and encourage the children to try each kind of movement such as walking, running, hopping, spinning, crawling, or dancing.